T0053075

BOOK OF BEGINNING TUBA SOLOS

Edited by **Fred Mills** and **Ron Romm**
of The Canadian Brass

■

All Selections Performed by
Charles Daellenbach on tuba,
and pianist Bill Casey

■

Plus Piano Accompaniments Only
Arranged by Bill Boyd

CONTENTS

The instrument pictured on the cover is a CB10 Tuba from The Canadian Brass Collection,
a line of professional brass instruments marketed by The Canadian Brass.

Photo: Gordon Janowiak

To access audio visit:
www.halleonard.com/mylibrary

Enter Code
2077-8806-3886-5238

Copyright © 1992 HAL LEONARD LLC
International Copyright Secured All Rights Reserved

For all works contained herein:
Unauthorized copying, arranging, adapting, recording, Internet posting, public performance,
or other distribution of the printed or recorded music in this publication is an infringement of copyright.
Infringers are liable under the law.

www.canadianbrass.com
www.halleonard.com

Dear Fellow Brass Player:

We might be just a little biased, but we believe that playing a brass instrument is on of the most positive activities that anyone can pursue. Whether you're 8 years old or 60 years old, the ability to play a horn automatically creates opportunities of playing with other people in bands, orchestras and ensembles throughout your life. But to keep yourself in shape and to better your playing, it's important to regularly work at solos. You might perform a contest solo for school, or play for a church service, or just for your family in the living room. Here's a book full of solos, in varied styles, that we think you'll enjoy learning.

All this music has been recorded for you on the companion audio. First, each of us in The Canadian Brass has recorded all the pieces in this collection on our respective instruments, letting you hear how the music sounds. Second, you will find piano accompaniments for you to use in your practice, of it you wish, to perform with. The recording of the solos that we have made should be used only as a guide in studying a piece. We certainly didn't go into these recording sessions with the idea of trying to create any kind of "definitive performances" of this music. There is no such thing as a definitive performance anyway. Each musician, being a unique individual, will naturally always come up with a slightly different rendition of a piece of music. We often find that students are timid about revealing their own ideas and personalities when going beyond the notes on the page in making music. After you've practiced for weeks on a piece of music, and have mastered all the technical requirements, you certainly have earned the right to play it in the way you think it sounds best! It may not be the way your friend would play it, or the way The Canadian Brass would play it. But you will have made the music your own, and that's what counts.

Good luck and Happy Brass Playing!
The Canadian Brass

CHARLES DAELLENBACH, tuba player in The Canadian Brass, graduated from Eastman School of Music at the age of twenty-five with a Ph.D. in music education. He then joined the music faculty at the University of Toronto, where he was head of the brass division. In 1970 collaborating with trombonist Eugene Watts, he helped found The Canadian Brass. The group became so successful so quickly that he soon had to devote his full time to performing and touring with the quintet. Charles' many interests have led him to become the businessman of The Canadian Brass, working closely with their managers, agents, lawyers, recording companies, and public representatives, as well as directing the group's ambition publishing activities. Charles is a natural on any stage, and is the quintet's quick-witted elocutionist.

BILL CASEY, pianist, grew up in Atlanta, and holds degrees in piano from Louisiana State University and the University of Missouri and Kansas City, He was assistant editor on the G. Schirmer Opera Anthology, and has recorded several other albums for Hal Leonard. He resides in Kansas City, where he runs a music school for piano and voice students, as well as continuing to perform as both a pianist and singer.

CANADIAN BRASS BLUES

Bill Boyd

Copyright © 1992 HAL LEONARD PUBLISHING CORPORATION
International Copyright Secured   All Rights Reserved

YANKEE DOODLE

Traditional American

Copyright © 1992 HAL LEONARD PUBLISHING CORPORATION
International Copyright Secured   All Rights Reserved

STREETS OF LAREDO

American Folksong (adapted from old Irish air)

Copyright © 1992 HAL LEONARD PUBLISHING CORPORATION
International Copyright Secured   All Rights Reserved

ODE TO JOY

Adapted from Symphony No. 9
by Ludwig van Beethoven

Copyright © 1992 HAL LEONARD PUBLISHING CORPORATION
International Copyright Secured   All Rights Reserved

AMERICA

Words by Samuel F. Smith
Music by Henry Carey

Copyright © 1992 HAL LEONARD PUBLISHING CORPORATION
International Copyright Secured   All Rights Reserved

CARNIVAL OF VENICE

Julius Benedict

Copyright © 1992 HAL LEONARD PUBLISHING CORPORATION
International Copyright Secured   All Rights Reserved

THE RIDDLE SONG

English ballad

Copyright © 1992 HAL LEONARD PUBLISHING CORPORATION
International Copyright Secured   All Rights Reserved

FINLANDIA

Jean Sibelius

Copyright © 1992 HAL LEONARD PUBLISHING CORPORATION
International Copyright Secured   All Rights Reserved

CANADIAN BRASS BLUES

TUBA

Bill Boyd

Copyright © 1992 HAL LEONARD PUBLISHING CORPORATION
International Copyright Secured   All Rights Reserved

YANKEE DOODLE

Traditional American

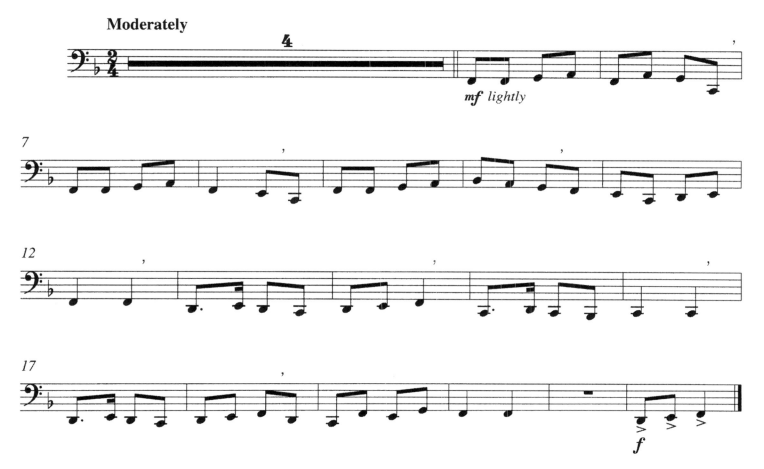

Copyright © 1992 HAL LEONARD PUBLISHING CORPORATION
International Copyright Secured   All Rights Reserved

STREETS OF LAREDO

American Folksong (adapted from old Irish air)

Copyright © 1992 HAL LEONARD PUBLISHING CORPORATION
International Copyright Secured   All Rights Reserved

ODE TO JOY

Adapted from Symphony No. 9
by Ludwig van Beethoven

Copyright © 1992 HAL LEONARD PUBLISHING CORPORATION
International Copyright Secured   All Rights Reserved

AMERICA

Words by Samuel F. Smith
Music by Henry Carey

Moderately

Copyright © 1992 HAL LEONARD PUBLISHING CORPORATION
International Copyright Secured   All Rights Reserved

CARNIVAL OF VENICE

Julius Benedict

Moderately

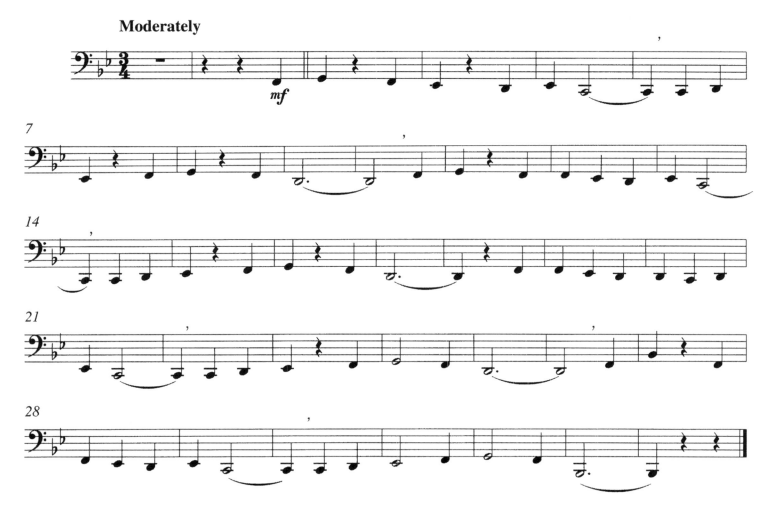

Copyright © 1992 HAL LEONARD PUBLISHING CORPORATION
International Copyright Secured   All Rights Reserved

THE RIDDLE SONG

English ballad

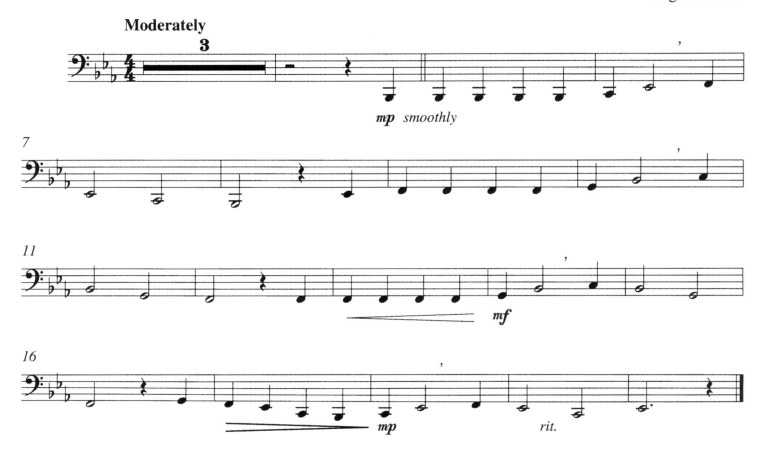

mp *smoothly*

mf

mp

rit.

Copyright © 1992 HAL LEONARD PUBLISHING CORPORATION
International Copyright Secured   All Rights Reserved

FINLANDIA

Jean Sibelius

mp *legato*

mf

mp

Copyright © 1992 HAL LEONARD PUBLISHING CORPORATION
International Copyright Secured   All Rights Reserved

AMAZING GRACE

Words by John Newton
Traditional American melody

Copyright © 1992 HAL LEONARD PUBLISHING CORPORATION
International Copyright Secured   All Rights Reserved

THE SKATERS

Emil Wauldteufel

Copyright © 1992 HAL LEONARD PUBLISHING CORPORATION
International Copyright Secured   All Rights Reserved

MARINE'S HYMN

Words by unknown marine (1847)
Music by Jacques Offenbach

Copyright © 1992 HAL LEONARD PUBLISHING CORPORATION
International Copyright Secured   All Rights Reserved

TAKE ME OUT TO THE BALL GAME

Words by Jack Norworth
Music by Albert von Tilzer

Copyright © 1992 HAL LEONARD PUBLISHING CORPORATION
International Copyright Secured   All Rights Reserved

SONG OF THE VOLGA BOATMAN

Russian Folksong

Copyright © 1992 HAL LEONARD PUBLISHING CORPORATION
International Copyright Secured   All Rights Reserved

THE CRUEL WAR IS RAGING

American Folksong

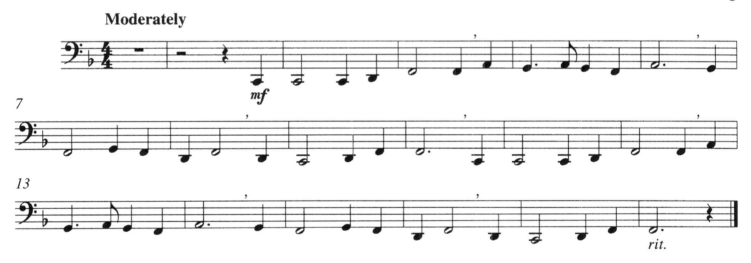

Copyright © 1992 HAL LEONARD PUBLISHING CORPORATION
International Copyright Secured   All Rights Reserved

DOXOLOGY

Words by Thomas Ken
Music by Louis Bourgéois

Copyright © 1992 HAL LEONARD PUBLISHING CORPORATION
International Copyright Secured   All Rights Reserved

GIVE MY REGARDS TO BROADWAY

Words and Music by George M. Cohan

Copyright © 1992 HAL LEONARD PUBLISHING CORPORATION
International Copyright Secured   All Rights Reserved

JUST A CLOSER WALK

Words and Music by Red Foley

Copyright © 1992 HAL LEONARD PUBLISHING CORPORATION
International Copyright Secured   All Rights Reserved

AMAZING GRACE

Words by John Newton
Traditional American melody

Copyright © 1992 HAL LEONARD PUBLISHING CORPORATION
International Copyright Secured   All Rights Reserved

THE SKATERS

Emil Wauldteufel

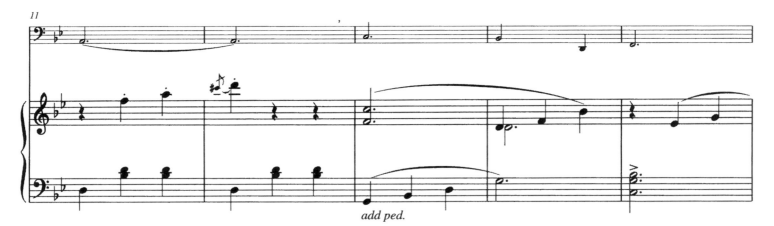

Copyright © 1992 HAL LEONARD PUBLISHING CORPORATION
International Copyright Secured   All Rights Reserved

MARINE'S HYMN

Words by unknown marine (1847)
Music by Jacques Offenbach

Copyright © 1992 HAL LEONARD PUBLISHING CORPORATION
International Copyright Secured   All Rights Reserved

TAKE ME OUT TO THE BALL GAME

Words by Jack Norworth
Music by Albert von Tilzer

Copyright © 1992 HAL LEONARD PUBLISHING CORPORATION
International Copyright Secured   All Rights Reserved

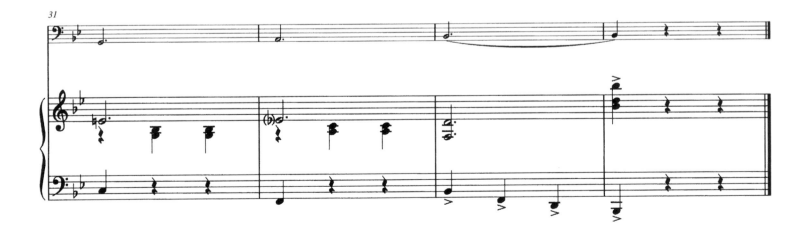

SONG OF THE VOLGA BOATMAN

Russian Folksong

Copyright © 1992 HAL LEONARD PUBLISHING CORPORATION
International Copyright Secured   All Rights Reserved

THE CRUEL WAR IS RAGING

American Folksong

Copyright © 1992 HAL LEONARD PUBLISHING CORPORATION
International Copyright Secured   All Rights Reserved

DOXOLOGY

Words by Thomas Ken
Music by Louis Bourgéois

Copyright © 1992 HAL LEONARD PUBLISHING CORPORATION
International Copyright Secured   All Rights Reserved

GIVE MY REGARDS TO BROADWAY

Words and Music by George M. Cohan

Copyright © 1992 HAL LEONARD PUBLISHING CORPORATION
International Copyright Secured   All Rights Reserved

JUST A CLOSER WALK

Words and Music by Red Foley

Copyright © 1992 HAL LEONARD PUBLISHING CORPORATION
International Copyright Secured   All Rights Reserved